Education Is Not Enough

Education Is Not Enough

Empowering Yourself for Success in the Real World

by

Imorataria Dogood Akpufu

Education Is Not Enough

(Empowering yourself for success in the Real World)

by Imorataria Dogood Akpufu

ISBN-13: 978-0993079245

Published by:
Father Abraham Publishers
3 Robinson Street, South Shield
NE 33 4PR, UK
Tel: +447714619964
Email: fatherabrahampublishers@gmail.com

Printed in the United Kingdom

Contact The Author At:
Nigeria Maritime University,
Okerenekoko, Delta State
Nigeria

Tel - +234-806-573-4966
Email – akpufu_i@yahoo.com

federal republic of Nigeria

Dedication

First, this book is dedicated to God Almighty, for His enabling strength He bestowed upon me, and for inspiring my heart to see education's challenges treated in this book as a problem that needs attention.

Secondly, I dedicate this book to my beloved students in Nigeria Maritime University, and those whose lives this book will prevent from repeating the same mistakes. It is also dedicated to those who think it is too to correct their mistakes because the book will inspire them to look inwards and aspire for a new hope, dream, and fulfilment.

Acknowledgments

I am most grateful to God Almighty for His unfailing love, protection, mercies and help I got from the editor, Shafe Ewuola, throughout the period of writing this book. I would like to express my sincere gratitude to several individuals for supporting me through my journey thus far. I wish to express my sincere gratitude to my destiny catalyst, pastor Joseph Possibility Omoragbon, and his team who offered timely criticism, patience, insightful comment, practical advice and corrections that have tremendously helped in writing this book. I could not have imagined having a better team because without your support and guidance, this project would have not been possible.

Secondly, my deepest appreciation goes to my parents, Madam Obebhatein Jonathan; my grandmother, for her labour of love from my infant age till date; my great grandma mama, Eunice Afeni, for overseeing the process of my growth and development with her dogged approach in ensuring change was possible; my big daddy and former Nigerian President, Dr Goodluck Ebele Jonathan, for his light in our lives who believe education is the way forward and a requirement of society; his lovely wife, Dr Patience Jonathan, for her support; my father Oguansi Dogood Akpufu, for my existence on earth; his siblings, Azibanayeluan Omonibeke and family for running around with me to Ensure smooth processing of my documentation during my school times.

I appreciate His Royal Highness (HRH), Miruobebh Dogood Akpufu, for the father figure role he plays in my Life and his admirable, Godgiven wife, Mrs Ediabai Akpufu, the one who we practically grew up together, for her beautiful presence in my life and for giving me niece and nephew who are like my siblings today; my maternal family for keeping and protecting me, especially Mr. Tunde, for support during my birth and toddler stage of growth, Inebharapu Napoleon Onyemaechi and family, Opaminola Johnson, for their words of encouragement, financial support and love.

I appreciate the Nigeria Maritime Administrative and Safety agency for the scholarship to study Nautical Science abroad; Mrs Irene Macfoy, for her care, Mr.

Patrick Obah, for the scholarship opportunity. The Nigeria Seafarers Development Programme batch O7 for their support; and my school mates - Olumide Bolarinwa Ajayi, for his financial support; my best friend, Mrs Cremelda Thomas from Sierra Leone, Mrs Ameera Syafiqah from Malaysia, Syed Baqir Ali Gardezi from Pakistan, Ahmad Fathy Abdalaal from Egypt, Kelvin Palama for a great time outside school in Liverpool.

To living faith church, South Shields; Garden of hope church in Liverpool and their respective pastors: pastor Joseph Possibility Omoragbon and Pastor Funmi Ilensanmi. St Stephen's Anglican Church Otuoke, thank you for the opportunity to serve in different capacities during my time with you all; the Falades and Fashinas for sharing your family and food with me; the Nigeria Maritime University, Okerenekoko, Delta State, for the opportunity to serve, the Port Management department and the entire faculty of transport and logistics management, I say thank you.

To my new families I got in life, the Adekolas for their warm embrace, the Etim family for their love; Mr Adekola Kehinde Adeyanju, for his role in my educational journey, Favour Orji Okeke and husband, for their assistance in my research work; the Amazon Network for the daily self-development and the amazing sisters that are always willing to help; to my friend turned sister, Comfort Etim Adewale, for allowing me to be myself and loving me unconditionally, I say thank you.

Contents

Endorsements

Endorsement by Ven. Justice G. M. Ikiogha

"Imorataria Dogood Akpufu has the transformational key to teach that without God, any schooling career or purpose becomes meaningless and a wanting vanity."

Endorsement by Dr Benefit Onu

"Education Is Not Enough", by Imorataria Akpufu, is a wonderful inspirational book that should not be missed to read by young people and parents who desire to set their future and those of their children aright."

Endorsement by Joseph Possibility Omoragbon, Snr. Pastor, RCCG Living Faith, South Shields, UK

"I enjoyed reading Taria's book 'Education Is Not Enough.' The book is raw, daring, and simple to comprehend.

Although some people may consider the book's content controversial, I agree entirely with the author's view because it applies to me in many ways, whether as an entrepreneur, educationist, minister of religion, author, or publisher.

On the other hand, Taria's point of view is also supported by both the Holy Scripture and empirical research. It is written, "I have observed something else under the sun. The fastest runner doesn't always win the race, and the strongest warrior doesn't always win the battle. The wise sometimes go hungry, and the skilful are not necessarily wealthy. And those who are educated don't always lead successful lives". It is all decided by chance, by being in the right place at the right time." (Ecclesiastes 9:11 NLT)

Furthermore, recent research conducted by Stanford Research Institute attests to Taria's position. It posits that the profit made in any endeavour is determined by 12.5% education and 87.5% ability to deal with people.

It is no longer news that some things are not taught in secular schools. The author clearly explained this view in simple-to-read language. Her use of the lifestyle of Sigmund Freud to illustrate the limitations of education makes her claim indisputable.

The author is not against education, as education is the passport to the future, as postulated by Malcolm X, who could not write his name when he was sent to prison in 1946 but came out as one of the most eloquent speakers America has ever had because of his self-education during his incarceration.

If you want to know the things more important than education, I recommend this courageous masterpiece to you with all my heart."

Foreword

It is my honour most responsibly to be given the privilege of writing the foreword to this aptly titled book, **"Education is Not Enough."** Facts in this book are indications that also define education as a process of learning or imparting knowledge or skill that continues in life till death. Very true.

Like the author, I agree that true wisdom means seeking, knowing, and being reconciled with our Creator. And it should be in spite of climbing a whole lifetime ladder of educational attainments. Need we, therefore, idolize (worship) education? The answer here is a resounding no! Just remember to strike a balance by seeking God's face for divine guidance.

Before all this, the author had admonished parents/guardians to be careful in the choice of course/career for their children and wards as this could have a fundamental effect as a make or mar point in life, as it is the determinant factor to propel or pull back students in the school, especially at the college and university levels. If the choice is the one imposed rather than one of free will, then a conflict of erosion sets in that affects performance. And who should know better than the teacher that the author and my humble self as teachers represent?

Quotes and footnotes abound to underscore and drive home cogent points advanced severally in the book by the author. And like the author, I have also travelled to other parts of the world and experienced the differences in environment, home and abroad.

Still, nothing compares to the fulfilment one gets from being in the presence of God. Whether as a student, parent, or guardian and it doesn't matter your calling or vocation, the only source of escape from boredom or frustration, as recommended by the author in this book, which I also agree with her totally, is seeking God's face rather than finding distractions in drinking alcohol, substance abuse, smoking, partying, immorality, clubbing and a host of other vices and activities. This is because when pleasure moments pass, frustrations and sorrows actually resume. Hence, according to the author, idolizing education will make life frustrating and not worth living indeed.

Accordingly, there are hindrances to educational benefits which are equally treated rightfully in their measured proportion, even as variables in sub-titles. They include: Unstable Policy, Uncertain Future, Education Is To Make Money, The Myth That Any First Degree Is A Good Degree, The Illusion That Government Can Fund Schools and Poor Foundations and so on. These are all encapsulated as a drawback in Nigeria's guest for excellence in educational achievements either in the national and international reckoning as well as in global rating, which at the moment sees us as a nation-leading shamefully from the rear, even in the comity of Banana Republics of the African sub-region.

The author equally encapsulated the virtues of continuous education, which helps in garnering experience even out of school and after the schooling environment.

The author also reminded us that a country like Nigeria that is failing in proper education policy vis-a-vis the purpose of education, where there is a conflict between the two, is an indicator that the government is operating at a level where a certificate is more important than its holder.

Finally, the place of career guide/counseling, which the author correctly observed to have lost its place in Nigeria's educational system, got a mention in the book. According to the author, the place of the profession of career counselling guides is to help students with guidelines on choosing appropriate programs of study.

In addition, they also encourage students to change or leave one program for another after an objective evaluation of their potential, weaknesses, strengths, and passions. Thus, they advise students accordingly and encourage them to make a decision that best suits their personalities and potential.

This tip and many others are why the book, “Education is Not Enough,” brings to the table that which makes it an essential companion, reminding one conclusively that education being a lifelong endeavour is never enough as one should continue to get an education until one dies.

Dr Asiam Blessing Ikuru
Permanent Secretary, Civil Service Commission
Bayelsa State

Introduction

My years of experience as a lecturer in Nigeria's higher learning institutions have allowed me to discover the sadness and frustration of most students.

Within their first year on the campus, most of them begin to manifest apathy for learning, and just a few of them manage to sustain their courage for a little longer before their interest also relapses and rests. While these students' core career curve is lowering, many find temporary fulfillment in socialization rather than studying.

Students face conflicts with their parents when pursuing passions and preferences different from parental expectations.

There are different reasons for this behaviour, as I discovered through my interaction with some of them. Nevertheless, the alarming trend of learning apathy among scholars presumed to be the future of a nation is worrisome. For some, they are in school to 'please their parents'. Others are in school because their peers are.

It is very typical of the African culture where children's achievements, including having an academic edge over their peers, rub their parents' egos. In such cases, parental pressure accounts for a significant percentage of why these students are in school. Some parents choose the course and the institution that befit their pride, irrespective of their children's goals, interests, aptitude, and choices.

Students face conflicts with their parents when pursuing passions and preferences different from parental expectations. The fast-thinkers among them evolve a means to the end by choosing the 'money-making' path over passion and purpose. The trouble with this outcome has many angles, one of which is the sheer waste of parents' investments in their children's careers.

For the students, the tendency to be drifters becomes very high. They flow with the tides, hoping to catch a lucky moment to make money. This attitude makes them highly vulnerable to vices of all kinds.

Finding themselves on a career path, somewhere off their interest tangent, they lack the motivation to invest their best in it. These students only read to pass their exams if there is anything worthwhile. Some don't even have enough drive to read and pass their exams. Instead, they court the friendship or favour of their lecturers for marks.

Sex and money for marks in an examination are trending shamefully. If everything else fails, they find a way to bribe their way through their career ladders. The female students draw confidence in their extra weapon of 'sex for marks.' Altogether, learning institutions keep releasing generations of graduates, whose career years are more like tourism, into a nation searching for tomorrow's leaders.

The other extreme to this educational problem is those who make an 'idol' out of their careers. They are devoted, studious, and highly ambitious scholars. So committed and focused are they that they can't spare God a moment of their lives. Self-development becomes their thin god with mighty influence on their lives.

Both cases require a reassessment and re-invention. With the failure of career guides in secondary schools in Nigeria, where the skills of graduates who provide guidance and counseling services are out of demand in nearly all the public schools, it is understandable that parental pressure and choices may prevail over the students.

However, this can be corrected through a unique career orientation program that will redirect the students' career paths. For 'worshippers' of their careers, the balance they need is that no education is complete, which does not inculcate the knowledge of God.

> *The core message of this book is that educational pursuit alone is incomplete to build a godly character.*

Education doesn't deliver much without knowing and using it as a tool in life. The fact that highly educated persons still suffer and are frustrated is a call for concern. I have come to realize that education is not enough. Life's journey entails much more than. The aim here is to understand the place of education in youth development. Our pursuit should be subjected to God and His plan for us.

The core message of this book is that educational pursuit alone is incomplete to build a godly character. It takes much more than mere learning for an individual to function appropriately. This fact is the balance this book brings to parents, students, and youths.

The Bible warns that 'But beyond this my son, [about going further than the words given by one Shepherd], be warned: the writing of many books is endless [so do not believe everything you read], and excessive study and devotion to books is wearying to the body. Ecclesiastes 12: 12.

Secular education alone does not educate anyone for ultimate fulfillment both now and in the afterlife. Everyone needs God in every chosen career path.

Imorataria Dogood Akpufu,
October 2022

Education Without God Is Insufficient

Chapter 1

Education Without God Is Insufficient

Let me begin with a curious peep into the magnificent career of Sigmund Freud. The Austria-born neurologist, and researcher, was considered the most influential intellectual figure of his days. As the father and founder of Psychoanalysis, his theories and contributions to studies on human personality, the subconscious mind, dream, human psyche, and many more defined his works as classic.

Freud was known as a chronic smoker of the cigar. Disregarding warnings of its dire health consequences, he still smoked 20 cigars a day! Later in his life, he was diagnosed with malignant mouth cancer, for which Freud had 30 surgeries out of the 33 scheduled for him. The pain was so much that he could not have any more surgery.

For his extraordinary and excellent education, research, and educational success, he downplayed the knowledge of God and disparaged any attempt to expound the way of eternal life to him. Freud was an unrepentant atheist who described belief in God as a 'collective neurosis. By that description, he dismissed belief in God as a mere expression of phobia, obsession, or some insanity.

Having relocated to London, where he spent his last days at 83, Freud's soul was drawing closer to the brink of eternity. His life was about to end; a life of commotion, obsession with learning, and fame for developing prominent theories.

<u>There is always an end to everything. There is an end to every career and life, however brilliant or obscure</u>. As he was inching closer to another life, which he never believed in its existence, the desperation to face the unknown was evident in his last moments.

There is always an end to everything. There is an end to every career and life, however brilliant or obscure.

As his pain and misery worsened intensively, Freud persuaded a doctor friend to aid his suicide with pathetic last words. He said, "'Now it is nothing but torture and makes no sense anymore." His friend pitifully agreed to help end his misery and administered an overdose of morphine to his body. Freud died shortly after, and his soul plunged into the eternity he disbelieved throughout his career life.

Globally, Sigmund Freud's legacy is unrivaled in the sciences. His commitment to education, learning, and research ranks him higher than many accomplished scholars of his time and now. The major flaw in his quest for knowledge to benefit humanity was to have dismissed belief in God. He didn't die because he didn't believe in God; he died because death is inevitable for all.

Education without God is delusional. When death calls, our souls meet the same God we have been so educated to avoid and disbelieve. There was no solution to Freud's spiritual, mental, and bodily misery of everything that education could offer in his days. His glorious career years and sad ending depict the pattern, pain, and vain pursuit of education without God.

For all scholars, especially those obsessed with education, the Bible drops a warning note to check and balance our pursuits. While we should go all the miles to get an education, going much further to acquire the knowledge of God is better for life on earth and in eternity.

Ecclesiastes 12: 12:

But about going further [than the words given by one Shepherd], my son, be warned. Of making many books there is no end [so do not believe everything you read], and much study is a weariness of the flesh. (AMPC)

The statement above is a warning. The writer expressly says, '...*be warned.*' He warns that there is no exhausting the available library of books, and there is no end to the new knowledge contributions yet to come. Further than these, he warns that as essential and beneficial as reading or studying is, it causes severe mental and bodily fatigue.

Education is a rigorous exercise despite its attractive benefits. The Bible recommends a balance between secular and spiritual education to relieve us from the burden of the wearisome routine, saying in Ecclesiastes 12: 13 that:

All has been heard; the end of the matter is: Fear God [revere and worship Him, knowing that He is] and keep His commandments, for this is the whole of man [the full, original purpose of his creation, the object of God's providence, the root of character, the foundation of all happiness, the adjustment to all inharmonious circumstances and conditions under the sun] and the whole [duty] for every man. (AMPC)

The Original King James Version of the Bible renders the verse above as '*Let us hear the conclusion of the whole matter: Fear God, and keep his commandments: for this is the whole duty of man.*' The whole matter concludes that our quest for education, learning, reading, and studying must put God into the equation. Education without God is an exercise in futility.

> ***Education is a rigorous exercise despite its attractive benefits.***

According to the text, the whole duty of humanity is to learn about God, who graciously put us in the world He created. Our education should serve to better our lives and environment during our sojourn in this world, but acquiring the knowledge of God guarantees us an eternal life of bliss.

❖ Delusion and Dilemma

From my experience, a life without God is dangerous and challenging. The mental instability from dealing with humans, betrayal, offenses, and the fading memories of the good days can be overwhelming. I lacked peace, joy, purpose, hope, confidence, and happiness in my pursuit of education without God. I was in constant pain emotionally, physically, mentally, and financially. The weariness that education without God exerts was confirmed in my life.

I dwelt more on my pains and the things I lacked. Crying to sleep was a daily hobby. I always walked around as a victim of self-pity. I always wanted to share past negative stories to seek attention and support from places with nothing to give. I was a product of a battered inner life. Instead of focusing on the solutions, using the same energy to work hard for the things I wanted, I turned to profitless options.

How accurate are the words of the Psalmist, which describe the vanity of human pursuits without seeking God! He says:

Psalm 53: 2-3:

2. God looked down from heaven upon the children of men, to see if there were any that did understand, that did seek God.

3. Every one of them is gone back: they are altogether become filthy; there is none that doeth good, no, not one.

We look everywhere to make an educational impact, but God looks down from heaven to check if anyone is wise enough to put Him in the equation. Education without God is meaningless and unfulfilling. The knowledge of God will help you utilize the skills you've acquired in the right way. The right way here means for the greater course in impacting lives.

There is always a void in every soul and the yearning for more. Nothing but knowledge can ever satisfy it. The inability to grasp, comprehend, accept or surrender to the true knowledge of God causes constant frustration and stress. It doesn't matter what religion you profess or promote, and nothing can replace the unending internal crisis and frustration except peace with God through reconciliation with Him.

"Remember, God has defined the purpose of your creation. You will never be at your best until you accept, adapt, and identify with it." - Bishop David Oyedepo

The delusion and dilemma of life without God's knowledge are severe. Education is thought to be a means to a life of peace, inner confidence, and freedom from the fear of the unknown, especially when death is near. Experiences and confessions of dying souls have proved this assumption wrong. Caesar Borgia was an Italian nobleman and politician.

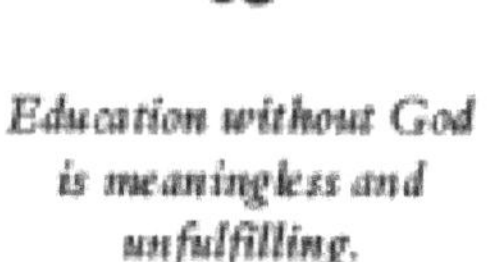

As a cardinal, he was religious but not reconciled with God to find the inner peace that guarantees eternity with God. In his last moments on earth, he lamented with the following words: 'While I lived, I provided for everything but death; now I must die, and am unprepared to die.'

Education empowers you to prepare for the best that life on earth can afford. It can bless you with an immortal name and fame, awards and rewards, money and mansions, wealth and earthly wisdom. However, the greatest shortcoming of education is that we never get educated enough to have everlasting life of unspeakable glory, except we consciously seek after God's knowledge. Education without God has no answer to your eternal destination after death.

Education without God derails one from God's purpose. You will be a wondering human on earth with a trial and error approach while wasting good time on needless things. Education puts you in life's competitive race and could make you see yourself as self-sufficient without God.

Listen to what a wise man says about the outcome of human efforts with God's offer:

> *The race is not for the swift ("I have observed something else under the sun. The fastest runner doesn't always win the race, and the strongest warrior doesn't always win the battle. The wise sometimes go hungry, and the skillful are not necessarily wealthy. And those who are educated don't always lead successful lives. It is all decided by chance, by being in the right place at the right time." Ecclesiastes 9:11 (NLT)*

God's offer to your efforts gives you a product above the value of your preparation. The Scripture above says something about timing, and indeed this is unpredictable. I have seen the best in class unable to attain what the average student has achieved over time.

Something supernatural can only happen to our lives through Jesus, which is essential in our pursuit in life. The true knowledge of God comes from accepting Jesus as Saviour and Lord. He is the light that makes all other forms of education appear like a cloud of darkness. I am neither the best in my class nor the most beautiful girl, but the things that have happened in my life can only be God.

❖ I Suffered Rejection and Depression

I was rejected while in the womb. The story caused me some depression. Out of fear, my Dad left my mom for Lagos after the news broke that she was pregnant with me. I lived without a dad for years before my grandmother decided to take me. You can imagine the trauma of growing up to know that you have a fugitive father.

I can still recall the first day he saw me and asked his mother, the grandma who took custody of me, whose child was I. In that environment, a lot happened that could have damaged my life. As I write this, there are pictures of events streaming through my mind. Even as a child, my situation looked hopeless before my grandma took me, but hope came not necessarily because it was better than others. My encounter with God through Jesus changed everything.

Today that abandoned little child with an absentee father has traveled to Europe, India, and the United Kingdom not because she's the most brilliant but by the grace of God. The Almighty God commended His love toward me long before my frustration and purposeless life brought me down on my knees. Jesus paid the price a long time ago. Down on my knees under the weight of my burden, I found Him right beside me.

Pursue knowledge but be wise enough to put God in the equation of your life.

He has always been there, but I did not acknowledge Him. I know how my life was without Him and what it is now with Him. I can boldly say God changed my life. Education has now become a handy tool for my purpose. Until you find your purpose in God, your education could be nothing but a mere adventure.

One of my testimonies is anchored on Romans 8:28 (KJV): *And we know that all things work together for good to them that love God, to them who are the called according to his purpose.*

I want you to take note of the words' *his purpose...*' in the text. Finding God's purpose for your life is the most significant discovery you can ever make. You should build your entire life on it as a foundation for your plans and pursuits. Your education isn't enough if it doesn't tally with His purpose. It is incomplete if it doesn't run as the vehicle of His purpose for your life.

Even though I did not plan as I should for lack of the proper guidance, Jesus always does the rerouting to get us to our original destination, just like the sat navigation system. That is the hope we have in Christ Jesus, and once you surrender to Him, He gets you back to his plans and purpose.

However, the time wasted has its consequences, but He uses them in His wisdom to accomplish His goal. Paul's encounter with Christ and His exploits after that prove that God can turn events around to achieve His purposes.

The importance of education cannot be overlooked, but there's more to life than education alone can offer. The Scripture below advises that we should not forget God in the days of our youth out of excitement.

> *Don't let the excitement of youth cause you to forget your Creator. Honor him in your youth before you grow old and say, "Life is not pleasant anymore."* Ecclesiastes 12:1 (NLT)

Being a youth has many excitements and ambitions attached to it. As a very delicate stage of life, it can rob you of seeking the knowledge of God and prepare you for an adult life born from the mismanagement of the youthful stage. Your old age is the sum of what your youthful energy was invested upon. Being busy does not equal hard work. Pursue knowledge but be wise enough to put God in the equation of your life. He changes everything.

2

Dangers Of Turning Education Into An Idol

Chapter 2

Dangers of Turning Education into an Idol

In my research, I found two dangerous extremes associated with education. The first is the conventional belief that education is the only road to competence. Proponents of this school of thought believe that a child's success graph rises or falls proportionally to their educational level. In every society, there are learning options; and the educational system is just one of them.

The belief that education is the only way a child can acquire the competence to succeed is faulty. The increasing success stories of many individuals who routed alternative learning options and gained the competence to compete and excel constitute a significant flaw to this belief.

My intention is not to bore you with examples of 'school dropout' entrepreneurs who found competence in alternative learning and attained a position of global influence. Some of them are among the largest employers of most culturally diverse labour across people globally.

An equally dangerous extreme is making an idol out of education. This school of thought puts the material world into the box of education and closes the mental windows to seek God. With some degree of educational fanaticism, the belief that education is everything about life makes it an idol. The libation of human time, talents, and resources is poured daily into its pursuit. This type of fanaticism is comparable to highly inflammable radical views in other areas of life that have pushed the world to its edge.

This school of thought considers the idea of God's existence and the need to seek Him as a lazy option and a denigration of the beauty of education. Supporters of this idea think that if God cannot be found through scientific and other educational research methodologies, the conclusion is that He does not exist. If by any chance He exists at all, He must be a mere distraction to human academic zeal and pursuits.

In some of its fields, education convinces us to believe that anything that does not fit into time, space, and matter is non-existent or inconsequential to human existence. Under the spell of this conclusion, we are programmed to spend a whole lifetime climbing various ladders of educational attainments without thinking about God, who gave us the blessings of space, time, and the material world.

My goal is to enumerate and prove the dangers of turning education into an idol. My method of doing it is to establish the futility of human labour without God's favour. Even if by any means anyone becomes successful, the reality of eternity in two different destinations awaiting humankind warrants that a wise choice has to be made while we live. True wisdom means seeking, knowing, and being reconciled with our Creator.

❖ An Idol Deprives Relationship with God

To clear the premises of this chapter idea, let me throw more light on the concept of 'idol.' Borrowing from the Jewish theology since they have the earliest organized system of divinity worship, idol worship is seen as a betrayal of relationship with God.

The word 'relationship' excited me during my studies because it captures everything the idea most succinctly. Consequently, anything that deprives, derails, or denies you of your relationship with God is an idol. Pursuing educational attainment without having the time for a relationship with God makes education an idol. As good as seeking academic achievement is, doing so at the expense of a relationship with God is idolatry.

With some degree of educational fanaticism, the belief that education is everything about life makes it an idol.

As Jewish theology expounds, idolatry has undergone evolutionary changes in concept and meaning. Continuous expansion and application of its meanings introduce a more expansive view of its meaning. In the light of this, idolatry is further defined as a wrong metaphysical projection.

Philosophy teaches that metaphysics is a word derived from two units – 'meta' (beyond) and 'physical' (the visible or material world). When the two units are combined to form the word 'metaphysics,' it means something beyond the physical or material world.

If idolatry is a wrong projection into a realm beyond the physical or material world, education is a significant projection gate. Extending human reasoning, imagination, and mind beyond the physical world into the sublime realms of existence is not wrong. Doing so is an exercise that classifies us as geniuses if our projections target the right subjects and goals.

A metaphysical projection is idolatry if it does not connect us with God. It is idolatry if it denies the existence of God. The worship of images believed to be physical symbols of invisible personalities is a wrong metaphysical projection. Occult practices, spiritism, divination, enchantment, and the use of incantations to control events and people in the material world take their origin from wrong projection into the spiritual realm.

What happens when education is turned into an idol? What happens if we are preoccupied with education without a place for God in our hearts and lives? The Bible drops a pathetic submission on the vanity of any pursuit without involving God. I summarized the Bible text under two sub-headings below:

❖ The Worst Can Happen to The Best

You can put your best into your goal and still have the worst outcome. We quickly dismiss this shared human experience as 'one of those things in life.' Yes, it is one of those pathetic and avoidable things in life. Through this experience, God wants us to admit and learn about human limitations. When your best fails to achieve its goal or your best earns you the worst, God wants you to know that there is something more than your best.

> ***You can put your best into your goal and still have the worst outcome.***

Despite putting in the best efforts, having the worst outcome could be seen as a providential educational tool to tutor us on the need to connect our actions with God's support. Anything with God's hand involved is failure-proof a hundred percent. Even with the best educational attainment, we are still vulnerable and insufficient in ourselves. Here is the submission of God's word:

Psalm 127: 1-2:

1. Except the LORD build the house, they labour in vain that build it: except the LORD keep the city, the watchman waketh but in vain.
2. It is vain for you to rise up early, to sit up late, to eat the bread of sorrows: for so he giveth his beloved sleep.

The above text begins with '*except,*' which carries a sense of exclusion. We are introduced to what happens to human labour in any field, including education, when God is excluded. The fields of building construction and security of life and property are only two examples to explain the wisdom of the text. Generally, the truth of the scripture covers all human activities.

The next important word in the text is 'vanity.' It occurs in its variant form as '*vain*' in the passage. By connecting the ideas of 'exclusion' and 'vanity,' we are immediately warned that whatever we do that excludes God is in vain. It may begin as a laudable project or a lofty ambition, but its exclusion of God in the equation makes everything a fruitless pursuit. Anyone who doesn't want to live a life of vanity or pursue education in vain must include God in the whole process.

As the Bible passage indicates, we '*...labour in vain...*' when we remove God from the equation of our endeavours. The word 'vain' is mentioned three times in the text. It is mentioned twice in the first verse and once in the second verse. But when we look at its linguistic influence in the opening clause, which says, '*It is vain for you to rise up early...*' we can safely conclude that the same sense of vanity is transmitted to the subsequent clauses.

Let me break this down further, though my expertise is in Maritime. I hope my colleagues in the academic world who specialize in English language or linguistics will pardon me for delving into their territory in this case.

Back to the original text, which says, '*It is vain for you to rise up early, to sit up late, to eat the bread of sorrows: for so he giveth his beloved sleep,*' we can reconstruct this sentence by putting it as shown below. With this modification, we can now see that the word 'vain' exists five times in the text.

- ✓ *It is vain for you to rise up early*
- ✓ *It is vain for you to sit up late*

- ✓ *It is vain for you to eat the bread of sorrows*

The Bible mentions' vain' five times to describe human labour with God's favour in a text of such few words. Vain is stated three times and implied two times in the text. This linguistic construct suggests that it is evident that without God, your education is insufficient, or your best efforts still producing the worst results imply that you need God's blessings on your endeavours.

Let's start with the first part of human vanity we face when we remove God from the equation. It says that rising early in life or rising early in time to pursue education is vain without God in the equation. As a learner, scholar, or researcher, the Bible says human efforts are in vain without God, however early in the stages of life or early in time your efforts may be.

Even with the best educational attainment, we are still vulnerable and insufficient in ourselves.

Waking up early in the morning to study without God's blessing is insufficient. Without God's blessings on your efforts, waking up early to start a career life is vanity. Waking up at an early stage in life amounts to nothing without God's blessings and favour.

Furthermore, the Bible says it is vain to '*...sit up late.*' Staying awake to read is one thing; understanding and retaining what is read is another. Processing what is retained and reproducing it creatively to solve human problems is a genius feat. Without God, it is vain to burn the hours of staying awake. Your best may still not be good enough. For those whose best efforts earn them the best results, it is vain to have the best without being sure of entering into God's rest after this world.

The third part of the vanity of human efforts without God is implied in the statement, '*It is vain for you to eat the bread of sorrows.*' The Bible uses '*bread of sorrows*' to describe insufficient, meager, or non-nutritional meals.

The expression' *bread of sorrows,*' '*no pleasant bread*' or 'bread of affliction' is used to describe the food eaten during some kind of Jewish fast, like when Daniel said, '*I ate no pleasant bread, neither came flesh nor wine in my mouth, neither did I anoint myself at all, till three whole weeks were fulfilled.*' Daniel 10: 3.

The expression also describes the kind of food given to prisoners like Micaiah when the king said, '...Take

Micaiah, and carry him back unto Amon the governor of the city, and to Joash the king's son; 28. And say, Thus saith the king, Put this fellow in the prison, and feed him with bread of affliction and with water of affliction, until I come in peace.' 1 Kings 22: 27-28

In the context of its usage above, '*It is vain for you to eat the bread of sorrows*' means denying yourself good food, nutritional meals, or sufficient food to achieve something important. Some people do that. They become austere to themselves in pursuit of their ambition.

Nevertheless, the word of God warns that self-imposed punishments, denials, pains, and malnutrition don't always guarantee success. People still die going through these processes. And others who survive it still have to hope that they have a long life and good health to enjoy the fruits of their labour. That is where God still comes in. At the beginning or the end of anything we do, we will always discover the need for God. He is the beginning and the ending:

Revelation 1: 8:

"I am Alpha and Omega, the beginning and the ending, saith the Lord, which is, and which was, and which is to come, the Almighty."

God's title as the Alpha and Omega, the Beginning and the Ending, puts His presence and influence in the three phases of time in the human world. He is the Lord who 'was'; He is God who 'is' and the King who 'is to come.' His power and reign cover the past, the present, and the future in the calendar of human existence. Wisdom demands that we seek Him and partner with Him throughout our lifetime.

We may forget Him somewhere in the past; He is here in the present. And if we ignore Him today, He is waiting for us in the future, whether we are alive or dead. There is no escaping the hands of the Most High God. Making an idol out of our education is misleading and eternally dangerous.

❖ Idolizing Education Is Frustrating

Psalm 127:1-2 summarizes my story. I have been in church almost all my life, but I never understood the basics of the importance of God. I saw Him as only a problem solver. So when everything was going well, I was nowhere to be found in His kingdom, and when life became unbearable, I ran to Him.

My move wasn't bad though, but it wasn't good enough as far as relationship with God is concerned. I commend my great-grandma and grandma for their godly influence on me, without which any alternative action could have taken me to a dangerous path with damaging effects.

The message here is that education is valuable and vital to our lives, but pursuing it without God or idolizing it will not lead to fulfillment. That was my personal experience. The idea that education is the answer to our entire problems was sold to me at home, and accepting it made me idolize it. I never bothered to develop my spiritual life, which my education should have enhanced.

As a student, spending long hours reading and studying can be tedious. I tried that in the past and experienced boredom and loss of interest. The experience could lead to apathy and an inability to achieve one's educational goal. I engaged in other activities outside school, which served as distractions. I felt refreshed when I returned to my books, but the vacuum in my spirit remained unfilled. A relationship with God is the only thing that can fill the emptiness in human souls.

Whenever I didn't go for other activities, I discovered the benefits of going for a walk once I was tired of reading. If I didn't go out for a walk, I went shopping. While studying overseas and up to date, my favourite activities include going for a long walk, shopping, and travelling by train. These got me relaxed and refreshed, unlike air transport.

Knowing how to choose my recreational activities helped me during my Master's degree days. I am forever grateful to my family, especially; my grandmother, for the opportunity God used her to create for me to attend World Maritime University Malmo" Sweden. Again, my recreation and the modern study environment of Sweden couldn't replace the hunger for God.

After acquiring knowledge and learning from my previous school experiences, I can say that studying in Sweden remains the best time of my life. I didn't have to wait for anyone to enjoy anything I found interesting or anything I wanted to experiment with.

I travelled and met people. I interacted with Colombians, Mexican, and Americans. We enjoyed some dinners together and had some drinks too. It was fun and worthwhile. Reflecting on the experiences now, none of the socialization exercises could take God's place.

> ∞
> ***The message here is that education is valuable and vital to our lives, but pursuing it without God or idolizing it will not lead to fulfillment.***

Idolizing education is frustrating. Apart from creating a false sense of satisfaction, which nothing but fellowship with God can fulfill, a religious pursuit of education is boring and frustrating. Its mental exaction is unimaginable. There could be the argument that my conservative background affected my social life. Some may even say that my passive attitude to adventures was responsible for my apathy to studies at some point.

In either case, I don't think so because I later discovered that true fulfillment and the inner joy that drives fulfillment come from a healthy relationship with God. We understand from the Bible that the strength we need to carry through comes from the joy of the Lord: '*for the joy of the LORD is your strength.*' Nehemiah 8: 10.

While studying at Malmö, my engagement in extra-curricular activities like exercising and eating healthy, besides working hard, reduced my frustration by some degrees. Any kind of distraction from the source of your frustration could give some sense of relief. The feeling of relief doesn't last forever. Once you disconnect from the distraction, the frustration resumes.

Temporary distractions from our frustrations don't remove them. Some find distractions in drinking alcohol, substance abuse, smoking, partying, immorality, clubbing, and a host of other vices and activities. When the pleasure moments pass, their frustrations and sorrows resume. In other words, idolizing education will make your life frustrating and not worth living.

Coping mechanisms will fail in the long run. They will lead you to quit or cause detours that could be too expensive. You will walk almost all the time with too much on your plate and heavy burdens on your shoulders. When you find a relationship with God, you find true satisfaction and fulfillment.

3

Benefits Of Education

Chapter 3

Benefits of Education

The benefits of education are diverse and inexhaustible. One of the most sensational stories illustrating the benefits of education is about the Guinness Book of the World Records holder, Nola Ochs, who bagged a university degree at the age of 95 in 2007. She graduated alongside her 21-year-old granddaughter. Ochs' dream was to become a storyteller on a cruise ship, so she majored in history.

She was the world's oldest university graduate until Shigemi Hirata, a Japanese, obtained a degree in Arts and Design at 96 years of age to beat her record. Ochs got her degree at Fort Hays State University (FHSU), Kansas, USA and Hirata got his at Kyoto University, Japan. Kyoto University ranks 127 on the list of the best global universities, the 16th best university in the whole of Asia, and the 2nd best university in Japan.

Ochs' derived many benefits from her educational career despite achieving the feat in her old age. She got fame and fulfillment. She enjoyed media appearances and spotlights. Her dream of becoming a storyteller on a cruise ship was eventually fulfilled as she was hired by Princess Cruises as a guest lecturer on a nine-day Caribbean Cruise. Ochs' case is strong proof that education has many benefits, no matter how late it is acquired.

Before she died at the age of 105 in 2016, Ochs added another feather to her career cap with a Master's degree. In 2007, she started pursuing her Master's in liberal studies at the same university where she obtained her first degree. She was awarded a Master's in 2010 to become the oldest recipient of a Master's degree at 98. At her 100th birthday, she was a graduate teaching assistant at the university. Education opens the door of many opportunities to those who value and pursue it with excellence. It's never too late at any age.

So in looking at the benefits of education, don't let us forget the advantages of the gift of life.

Ochs testimony gave credit to God when she said in an interview that 'I don't keep track of my age, but I can tell you I was born in November of 1911. I've led a long, interesting life. We went through the dust storms. We had some difficult times in our marriage, financially. But it's been the Lord's will that I've lived this long life, and I thank Him kindly for it.'

Can you see the point I have been trying to make? We can only dream and pursue our passions when we have the gift of life. Living that long allowed her to pursue her career dream. Life is a gift from God without which we cannot do anything.

So in looking at the benefits of education, don't let us forget the advantages of the gift of life. Before listing and explaining some of these benefits, let me remind you of an allegory in the Bible about a young man with a brilliant ambition who had remarkable success in his career path. He was successful but lost the gift of life to enjoy his success. Here is the story:

Luke 12: 16-21:

16. *And he spake a parable unto them, saying, The ground of a certain rich man brought forth plentifully:*

17. *And he thought within himself, saying, What shall I do, because I have no room where to bestow my fruits?*

18. *And he said, This will I do: I will pull down my barns, and build greater; and there will I bestow all my fruits and my goods.*
19. *And I will say to my soul, Soul, thou hast much goods laid up for many years; take thine ease, eat, drink, and be merry.*
20. *But God said unto him, Thou fool, this night thy soul shall be required of thee: then whose shall those things be, which thou hast provided?*
21. *So is he that layeth up treasure for himself, and is not rich toward God.*

The lesson in this parable is that the gift of life supersedes the benefits of our dreams. We need life to pursue, achieve and enjoy success. God is the giver of life. Every living soul is a debtor to the giver of life. We cannot set Him aside while pursuing our life's dreams. Now, on the benefits of education, let me share these with you:

- ✓ **Social Benefit**

I want to share my personal experience with you. As a child, I was shy to a fault in my early days. I could be described as someone with low self-esteem. The fear of the unknown was the reason for this experience. Fear is the worst enemy of faith. While faith makes you fly, fear fetters your feet to a spot.

Some fears are based on real situations, and other kinds of fear grow from assumptions. When the disciples of Jesus saw Him walking toward them on the waters, they were afraid; they feared for their lives because they assumed they saw a ghost. My assumption limited me and stopped me from growing.

Education makes you more sociable and broadens your horizon. One of the benefits of education is the wide range of individuals it makes you come across. My time at Liverpool John Moore allowed me to have friends from Malaysia, Egypt, Turkey, Pakistan, and Nigeria. I do not think that would be possible without education. My time at World Maritime University, which had students from across the world's continents, was a robust social benefit I derived from the pursuit of education.

No matter where you acquire yours, education improves your social life. Bringing you in contact with students from different backgrounds of cultures, traditions, religions, social classes, and economic power makes education rub on your social life with a significant impact.

Some fears are based on real situations, and other kinds of fear grow from assumptions.

Education makes you embrace the fact that no one is an island, and none should be. By mistake or choice, we recoil into a lonely world and risk falling into depression when we withdraw from healthy social life.

Some victims of suicide first manifest depression before taking their lives. A depressed life leads to isolation from social life. You find people like that getting progressively withdrawn from everyone. Education is meant to solve this problem by providing a level-playing ground for cross-cultural interaction in a racially and culturally diverse academic environment. You become better when you interact responsibly. Education gives you the greatest opportunity to do so.

Moreover, education gives you confidence among people. Confidence here is not arrogance. The confidence derived from education enables you to courageously admit it when you're wrong. For instance, you could wrongly cite references in an academic exercise.

If your facts and figures are correct except for the sources of information, there is no reason to lose self-confidence. Education helps you overcome an inferiority complex that prevents you from sharing your opinions with others.

✓ Economic Benefits

Another importance of education is that it paves the way for economic empowerment. It opens doors to opportunities. I want to add that education opens doors to ideas as well. Moreover, education helps you acquire skills that position you for good or better jobs.

There is a correlation between obtaining higher certificates and getting high-paying jobs or higher placement in the employment cadre. With higher education, you tend to rise higher and earn more.

For example, an edition of the United States Census Bureau reveals that a doctoral degree holder earns an average of $99,995 per year. The figure amounts to about N50 million at 1 dollar to 500 naira exchange rate. Holders of higher school diplomas earn an average of $33 618 in a year, about N17 million at the same exchange rate.

The First and Master's degree holders could earn an average of $60,954 and $71,236 per annum, respectively, which is N30 million and N35+ million per annum, respectively. In Nigeria, we are familiar with the civil service salary structures and how they differ depending on qualifications. The higher your education is, the better your chance of earning more.

✓ Human Capacity Development

Education makes you thoughtful and careful. In the 21st century, where people manipulate their way to get what they want, you must know what you want and work hard to get it. Education is a means for human capacity development. You are not in school only to obtain a certificate; you are in school to acquire knowledge and skills that will equip you for human capacity performance in the future.

> ***There is a correlation between obtaining higher certificates and getting high-paying jobs or higher placement in the employment cadre.***

Education is a development process. The difference between who you were before you got to school and whom you are after leaving school is the measure of your amount of education. Your certificate is less valuable than your skills. Flaunting a certificate your skills and knowledge cannot defend makes you appear ridiculous. Education makes you crave for development of your innate capacities.

✓ Healthy Competition

Education makes me compete healthily, making my mind clearer and more civil. Unhealthy competition has a link with a lack of education. Where it occurs among the educated, it means they act below the knowledge acquired. Lack of education causes unhealthy rivalry that sometimes degenerates into dangerous dimensions. Besides promoting healthy competition among learners and other members of society, education promotes good health among the educated. Educated people are more conscious of health hazards, and they tend to adopt a more hygienic way of life than uneducated folks. As an instrument for mental awareness, education increases mental consciousness of safety tips in matters of food, liquid consumption, and the use of medicine.

✓ Improved Productivity

Suppose two men are into the business of buying and selling. One is educated, but the other is not. Both of them have their shops next to each other. They don't display anything to reveal their educational qualification or lack of it. Soon, customers begin to troop in to buy their wares. By merely observing their approach to business, customer relationship, communication, business organization, and service delivery efficiency, you will agree with me that something about the educated guy will reveal his true identity.

<u>Education improves productivity in any business field.</u> Educated people tend to perform more than their uneducated counterparts. In any branch of business or industry, education introduces innovation that makes the business of the educated unique and more attractive. Uneducated business owners tap into the expertise of the educated ones to run and sustain their businesses because they lack something the educated people have.

Education can give you foresight. I have a big daddy that most people admitted could gain insight into their secrets, and they wondered how and why he could. As I grew, I understood it better. I didn't see it anymore as a mystery because I discovered that education enables you to predict most events accurately without consulting a soothsayer. Once you put on the analysis hat, you will definitely arrive at conclusions close to complete accuracy.

Education is wealth because knowledge comes in different forms and can turn your life around from zero degrees to 360 degrees. It makes you kind and loyal to people and prevents mismanagement of resources. Education safeguards against mismanagement and helps you to handle anything you do correctly. It leads you to success.

Education makes you develop a sound mind that won't get you easily swayed. I remember my dad lost a good amount of money to money doublers. Some might see the experience as resulting from greed, but I would rather say his level of understanding contributed to it.

My great-grandma was not educated, but she once said something I found to be factual. She said, 'if something is as good as people say it is, it would hardly get to you first. Others would keep it to themselves or families only.' For instance, if money doubling works, why wouldn't I manufacture my own money before telling anyone about it?

Education makes you more understanding and easy to relate with. It makes you stand out from others in the crowd.

Knowing well that life is a teacher, education makes you gentle and humble. No amount of education you get can be enough. I once heard that learning is a skill everyone should have because once you stop learning, you stop growing. With the pace of things these days, yesterday's lesson is outdated if not improved today. This makes you humble yourself in order not to make yourself ridiculous.

✓ Threats To Educational Benefits

A United Nations report on global education statistics and the impact of the Covid-19 pandemic reveals the need for urgent steps to safe, educational systems across the world. The benefits of education far outweigh its demerits, if there are any at all.

The report says that despite the efforts in the last few years to increase access to education, 260 million children were still out of school in 2018. The report says the figure corresponds to one-fifth of the global population of 7.592 billion in the same year. More appalling than this is that more than half of all children and adolescents worldwide have yet to meet the minimum proficiency standards in reading and mathematics, the report states.

Education improves productivity in any business field.

The temporary closure of schools due to the pandemic was said to have affected over 91% of students worldwide. As of April 2020, investigations and research on the effects of the pandemic indicated that about 1.6 billion children and youth were out of school. Out of this swelling figure, almost 369 million children worldwide who relied on school meals had to consider other sources for their daily sustenance.

The aftermath of the pandemic on present and future educational systems across the world calls for serious action because the world cannot afford to lose the benefits of education in every society. With the drastic setback in children and adolescents' education globally, the future benefits of education are dangling dangerously in the balance.

It is an understatement to say there is a need for urgent redemptive work through government, the private sector, and parents' collaboration. Each time an event disrupts a country's education, the implication is that all the benefits education brings are jeopardized.

The word of God expressly tells us in Proverbs 14: 23 that '*In all labour there is profit:...*' We labour in education to make and enjoy profits. Included in what the Bible calls profits are the numerous benefits that education brings, many of which I didn't list in this chapter but belong, one way or another, to the umbrella sub-topics treated above.

<u>Education is a kind of labour; it is not a pastime.</u> As a student or learner, you need to take it seriously but cautiously. The balance is that you must recognize God,

who gave you the gift of life and the scholastic aptitude to acquire knowledge in your chosen field. Together with God on the journey of educational careers, we are certain that our profits and benefits shall not elude us.

4

Our Educational Systems

Chapter 4

The Challenge of Unstable Educational Systems

The former United States Secretary of Education, Elizabeth Besty DeVos, would be remembered for many reforms she pursued in the country's educational systems. On an occasion of reviewing America's educational system, she said, '*Too many schools are operating "very similarly to 100 years ago, and the world today is much different.*'

As advanced as America's education systems are compared to others worldwide, describing them as operating 100 years behind today's demand dismisses the far more inefficient, disorganized, and ailing education systems in developing countries like Nigeria.

Meanwhile, in 2021 the US topped the list of the best country for education globally for a second consecutive year. While the US is home to eight out of the top best global universities, the United Kingdom came second in the same ranking, hosting two of the world's best universities. Germany, Canada, and France make the last three in a descending hierarchy. In Europe, the two countries are Germany and France; two are in North America, the US, and Canada; and one is in the UK.

It may surprise you that Nigeria is yet to make the list of the top ten African countries with the best education system, even as of 2022. Seychelles, a small island with less than one million people, tops the list of the best. The World Economic Forum rates the country with almost 70% points in its education. It makes the list of the top fifty best educational systems globally.

South Africa, Mauritius, Tunisia, Kenya, Algeria, Ghana, Egypt, Namibia, and Libya crossed the hurdles to make the list of the top ten best education systems in Africa, while Nigeria is struggling to retain its 124th position in the world and 25th in Africa behind Rwanda.

Chaos in students' life and future starts with the government's obsolete or ineffective education systems. I call this an institutional hindrance to achieving the benefits of education. Similar to this hindrance are policies or legal obstacles which stand in the way of flexible and rapid learning processes that put other countries ahead. The first and the worst barrier to deal with is the system of education that produces unproductive graduates.

❖ Unstable Policy, Uncertain Future

Nigeria has gone through successive regimes of educational policy change. Some of the changes make the nation's educational system sluggishly reel back and forth like a tired pendulum. In 1977, Nigeria published its first policy on education, which has gone through repeated reviews.

Thirty-seven years after experimenting with the original policy, the government wielded its power through the federal ministry of education and proposed that government would be responsible for primary education. The emerging approach made basic education compulsory and accessible for all. This policy directly or indirectly

The first and the worst barrier to deal with is the system of education that produces unproductive graduates.

fettered the hands of stakeholders in the industry, and the risk of ineffective delivery of educational services soared.

The new policy was structured as follows: one year was to cover pre-primary education to be followed by six years of primary education and three years of junior secondary education. The continuous evolution of the policy gave birth to the much-celebrated 6-3-3-4 formulation.

Learners would spend 1 year in pre-primary education and 6 years running primary school education. They will spend another 3 years pursuing the junior secondary school education, and the second 3 years for the senior secondary school education. After this, they continue with 4 years in the university, polytechnic, or their equivalents.

Again, this was subject to further review and adapted to suit the government curriculum. The continuously unstable educational policy leaves students, parents, and wards' future careers uncertain.

Facing an uncertain career future in an unstable educational policy framework, parents, wards, and students started developing learning apathy and wrong objectives. Coupled with the annual graduation of scholars with no absorption opportunities in the employment market, our educational system's failure started manifesting in various ways.

✓ Education Is To Make Money

I do not know where students got the idea that education would make them rich. Education is a means to the end and not an end in itself. It allows you to learn the skills to pursue your passion or accomplish a task of your future interest.

Education is, therefore, a tool that introduces you to a world of tasks that could make you rich. The best-paid employee in the world is not on the list of the wealthiest people in the world. Your education is a door to your dreams. Until you find your dream, you may not find fulfillment or riches.

✓ The Myth That Any First Degree Is A Good Degree

Education is not a fit-all-size mechanism for wealth creation. You need to research what educational programme best suits your dream. And it is essential to know that times have changed. The regular curriculum of educational institutions serves a common goal but to be exceptional, you need to be purposeful in your pursuit of knowledge.

> *Education is a means to the end and not an end in itself.*

A reputable media listed 30 university degrees or majors, considered the best future ranking in terms of employment opportunities and salary scales in the global market. The list includes petroleum engineering, cybersecurity, nuclear engineering, software engineering, physics, computer science, chemistry, economics, electronics engineering, information technology, health informatics, management information systems, and game design.

It continues with mechanical engineering, public administration, liberal arts, biomedical engineering, civil engineering, industrial engineering, construction management, communications, marketing, accounting, business administration, finance, management, nursing, political science, education, and English.

Among the degrees most demanded in 2021 were Pharmacology, Computer Science, Health Science, Information Technology, Engineering, Business Administration, Finance, Human Resources, Education, and Psychology. The usual institutions no longer serve societal needs but lay foundations to build on. As a student, you need to understand the demand in your immediate and global environment to find the right place for your career passion.

✓ The Illusion That Government Can Fund Schools

As a lecturer, I can tell you that government institutions lack the funds and resources to adequately cater to the required education of the day. The foreign institutions keep upgrading and adapting to new ways of development. But to stay in business and keep tuition affordable, they are also just a system ahead of public institutions. They are not of perfect or standard demands of industries but are much closer than the public schools.

Nigeria's 2021 budget for education was 6.3%. It has been criticized as the lowest in ten years! Out of the N11.7 trillion budget, only 742.5 billion was allotted to the education sector. N615.1 billion would go into recurrent expenditure, while N127.3 billion was left to take care of capital expenditure.

Every effective system adheres to a pattern that makes them successful. If we're sincere, the present-day standard of education is not comparable to the standard in my grandmother's days. This is not a blame game but a fact that must be acknowledged and addressed. I went to schools where there wouldn't be physics, English, and mathematics teachers for a session.

To fulfill all righteousness, a particular teacher would be assigned to take a specific topic and set an examination on it. There are extreme cases where

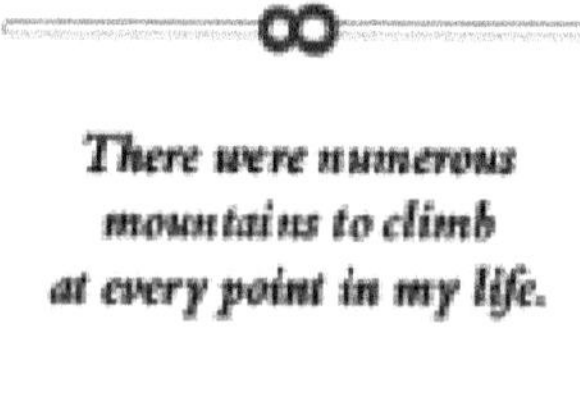

the school may have teachers who never attend classes because of their levels or whom they know in society. The heads of schools are compelled to protect them, and sometimes, tokens are given in the process. This practice goes on in most primary and secondary schools except for the latter, predominantly in public schools.

- ✓ **Poor Foundation**

Due to the ill-preparedness of most students in their foundational years in school, their performance in tertiary schools is never encouraging, and they end up hating and abusing educational systems. This is a dangerous situation that has subtly degraded the level of impact education used to have.

Imagine a scenario where you're advised that education is the only way out of life and you have to make the best use of its opportunities. Your zeal to achieve the best will get you mad at a dysfunctional system. I remember not enjoying school because everything came to me like a struggle. There were numerous mountains to climb at every point in my life. To succeed, you will keep doing extra work to better align and present yourself more appropriately. This is the dilemma of most students and graduates in Nigeria.

Even students and graduates in the above category are lucky because others cannot read and write after graduating from secondary school. Guess what? I have met those that could solve numerous mathematical equations if one would read for them. Unfortunately, most of the potentials in this part of the world are untapped or not enhanced. There are no provisions for students with special needs in our government schools. Persons with disabilities just waste their lives away for no greater crime than being Nigerians.

There is a high decline in standards in governmental schools these days. It is a place that will soon render our educational system worthless if nothing is done about it. The result will affect all other sectors in the country and our general wellbeing. Certificates speak louder than their owners because the owners cannot defend them. Building self-confidence on credentials instead of competence will continue to deplete the workforce and employable labour.

The private institutions are even worse in some aspects regarding the level of competence of their lecturers or teachers due to the enormous profit margins the owners want in their business endeavours. Management compromises the quality of staff members to keep their businesses running at low costs. And the better ones run at high fees that most students cannot afford. Because there are categories of students who cannot afford these schools, their parents keep pushing and begging for them to stay in the schools due to their advantages over public schools.

Some public schools have more competent lecturers and teachers without the equipment and resources to disseminate updated information and knowledge effectively. How about the level of payment they receive? It is a world of high knowledge but a low level of living. Self-development is hard to follow because of the less privileged and the funds available to this set of people.

This affects their performance in their various offices because mental work requires time and dedication. If they combine other endeavours outside the academics, the result becomes minimal knowledge servings, especially for the new and young lecturers.

Poverty is a contributing factor in the attitude of students in school. Passing an examination is not a good qualifier for education. Due to lack of funds, some students will be out of school long after resumption because they need work for money. They will join school weeks before exams and still do well.

The truth remains that their knowledge is just for passing an examination. The training required will be missing at a more significant cost in the future. However, some will voluntarily decide not to attend classes due to a lack of interest and good reason for going to school.

There's the issue of school resumption attitude in Nigerian public schools where the resumption date will need additional weeks for schools to stabilize. The above reason has affected the preparedness of parents and students.

Poverty is a contributing factor in the attitude of students in school.

In my early primary school days, resumption was never exciting because it took weeks for school activities to kick off. My mother being a teacher made it even worse for us. My grandmother was one of the prompt teachers in her days, and we had no excuse to stay back and wait for school to stabilize.

This really affected the journey ahead as a student. It was inbuilt into my system and became my expectation even as I grew older. My first days in the University abroad were a shock as lectures started on the resumption date after a week of orientation. Every activity was clearly stated and adequately planned for the academic session. The preparedness and precision of dates for activities abroad are worthy of emulation.

5

What You Do Not Learn From School

Chapter 5

There Are Things You Don't Learnt from School

The art of learning beyond the classroom and the school curriculum complements a successful life. A school can't teach you everything you need to know. The profound Greek philosopher, Socrates, emphasized the pursuit of knowledge throughout his lifetime.

He believed that for anyone to distinguish between right and wrong, people must exercise the power of reasoning to act in good conscience. Socrates believed the individual, not the society, has the responsibility to pursue the right thinking and proper behaviour through clear conscience. This branch of his philosophy puts the responsibility to acquire knowledge on everyone, and it extends the scope of learning beyond a single organized system like the school.

There are bodies of knowledge you will learn outside school. Beyond the classroom, there is a lot to learn from life's experiences. Jesus' disciples always sat with Him to learn in a classroom format. The great Teacher took them through the fundamentals of God's Kingdom principles and practices. They had a lot to learn more from experience outside the classroom.

- **Experience Is A teacher**

Experience is the result of applying acquired knowledge. It is also the outcome of not using acquired knowledge. Experience is produced from the application or non-application of knowledge. The experience itself becomes another window of knowledge to accept and appropriate. Therefore, every experience has a lesson to teach. We only learn from experience when we recognize and imbibe its lessons.

Jesus taught knowledge but left room for practical experience. If you are afraid to experience anything that providence brings your way, you are not prepared to acquire more knowledge yet. Jesus gave the disciples a mandate and how to deliver it. He was silent on what they would experience in the process. God allows experience to teach its lessons under His control and watch. Whatever your experience is, God is watching, and He is in control. Here is Jesus' account with His disciples:

Luke 10: 1, 17-20:

1. *After these things the Lord appointed other seventy also, and sent them two and two before his face into every city and place, whither he himself would come.*

17. *And the seventy returned again with joy, saying, Lord, even the devils are subject unto us through thy name.*
18. *And he said unto them, I beheld Satan as lightning fall from heaven.*
19. *Behold, I give unto you power to tread on serpents and scorpions, and over all the power of the enemy: and nothing shall by any means hurt you.*
20. *Notwithstanding in this rejoice not, that the spirits are subject unto you; but rather rejoice, because your names are written in heaven.*

Jesus' pattern follows a sequence that contains 'classroom' lessons, appropriate teaching methodologies, the disciples' opportunity for practical experience, and the lessons to learn from the experience. Having taught them what to do and how to do it, the disciples' next task was from their experience on the field. The incident added another curriculum to their knowledge acquisition.

What did they learn from the field experience? We can sum up what they learned in the following ways:

- Their experience validated their theoretical knowledge
- Their experience introduced success management Course
- Their experience drew their attention to priorities

Briefly, let me explain each of the three points above. Then I will apply these profound lessons to the discourse of this chapter.

- ✓ **Their Experience Validated Their Theoretical Knowledge**

On their return from carrying out the Master's mandate, they confirmed that what the Lord taught them on the power and authority of God's Kingdom was true. The demons' subjection to them through the

Lord's name validated His divine Sonship and authority over all creatures.

Before then, they knew that demons had power over humankind and could wreak havoc as they wished. But Jesus came and taught them that the authority of the Kingdom He came to present supersedes the authority of any other kingdom, either visible or invisible. Until they went out to prove His word through experience, they didn't know the power of the truth delivered to them in the classroom sessions.

The art of learning beyond the classroom and the school curriculum complements a successful life.

The school teaches bodies of knowledge contained in curriculums. They are principles to practice outside school. The validation of what is learned comes from field experience. To be successful in the field, a student has to follow the lessons learned from school meticulously. Much of the students' disappointing performances outside school result from failure to carefully and wholly apply the knowledge acquired in school.

✓ Their Experience Introduced Success Management Course

Out there, Jesus' disciples succeeded in their mission. They testified that the devils were subject to them at the mention of Jesus' name. Practicing the principles Jesus taught them yielded a huge success. Their excitement was understandable, but success was an experience they needed a new lesson to handle.

They had heard success stories and seen Jesus succeed in ministry. What they lacked was the practical, personal experience of managing success. Their experience was their chance to learn something new. After school, success, fame, wealth, and influence are possibilities. Field success could derail or destroy if management techniques are not applied.

✓ Their Experience Drew Their Attention to Priorities

Success in any endeavour creates new opportunities and management responsibilities. Breakthroughs, growth, and

Experience is the result of applying acquired knowledge.

expansion are achievable successes in the field. The new opportunities they bring make priorities rearrangement imperative. Wrong placement of priorities is one of the worst enemies of success. From the context of the reference, we can infer that Jesus saw how excitement could pose a threat to priorities.

Success excitement has caused wrong investment and partnership in business. Some have concentrated on the less important things because they are excited about the success of the big things. In their long history as Jews, they never saw where demons obeyed humans through the name of Jesus as it happened to them. We could say they broke new grounds in ministry as people do break new grounds in business. Their excitement was something we can associate with but cautioned their celebration.

We can learn how to succeed in school, but the experience will teach us success management in the field. Obviously, there are things we learn through experience. Many of these experiences are waiting for us outside the classroom. Some of them will validate our knowledge, and others will drive us back to seek more knowledge.

During my higher national diploma days in India, fear kept me from exploring the environment outside school. I thought indulging in extra curriculum activities would negatively affect my grades. That was a big lie! I regretted not making good use of the time to bond with my mates. Such time and opportunities are usually irredeemable.

The importance of building a good relationship is one thing nobody would teach you. Building a healthy social life will help you. Doing so does not mean that you have to tolerate people's excesses. Learning how to get along with as many people as you can afford is the rule. My current employment status resulted from reconnecting with a schoolmate at a business venture I dived into after graduation. Social life in school is different from social life outside school. Learning its principles at school helps its practice outside school.

❖ The Impact of Fellowship with Like-minds

Like-minds are people who share with you the same values, religious beliefs, principles of life, philosophies, and passions. The sociology of group formation suggests that individuals bond because of common interests. Their common interest is the core of their relationship.

I remember when I was running my bachelor's degree programme in Liverpool. Bonding with like-minds in the fellowship I attended helped my career days. I owe my success partly to the impact of fellowship with the brethren. Their warm interactions, encouragement, and prayers supported my career journey in ways beyond what I could quantify.

I lost my mom while away for studies, and I still remember vividly how I would find myself on the floor most days. I passed out because the shock was too rude and brutal. Some community persons were also in the United Kingdom, and they made efforts to assist me in pulling through the trying times. Each time they visited, I felt strong. But when they left, I felt weak and broken. During that period, my life went through weak and strong emotional seasons. It would have been worse, but for the support I got.

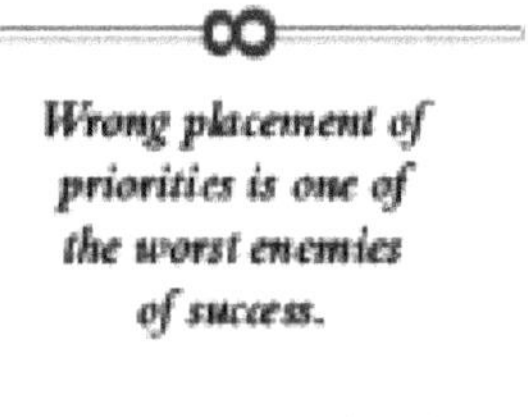

I was still a shadow of myself when I visited the Redeemed Christian Church of God (RCCG) branch called "Garden of Hope." I also met a lady called Comfort who opened the doors of her home to me. The church and the lady played different roles in my life, which were very helpful to my recovery and healing. The brethren invited me over and cooked food. I spent weekends with their families. Most times, we participated in different activities. The relationships helped me get through homesickness and loneliness.

❖ The Importance of Being Under Authority

The fellowship interactions did not just happen. It occurred as an extension of the warmth I got from where I was coming from in South Shields, United Kingdom, where I served under Pastor Joseph Possibility Omoragbon at Living Faith, another parish of the Redeemed Christian Church Of God (RCCG). I met a particular female pastor that linked me with brother AJibola in Liverpool when I went for further studies.

Since it was a new city, I knew no one there until I was introduced to the church that became my second home.

The connection would not be possible if I did not yield myself to the church's authority on every occasion. The church leadership took the responsibility of guardianship over me. Seeing me as a flock member, they ensured I was within the fold and extended care to me.

❖ The Art of Thanksgiving

Psalms 50:22-23 says, 'But giving thanks is a sacrifice that truly honours me. If you keep to my path, I will reveal to you the salvation of God.' NLT. If you want to learn more about the power and benefits of thanksgiving, I recommend reading "The Thankful Mother," a book by Joseph Omoragbon.

I like to add that thankfulness is a pathfinder. For gratitude to be cultivated in one's life, the power of reflection must be in place, and this act is a pointer to many areas of God's faithfulness. Thanksgiving helps you to review your spiritual life and benefits. God teaches and builds us at every phase of life, but many people dwell on the wrong things and are unthankful.

❖ Knowledge from The Elderly

There is a difference between education and the wisdom acquired from experience. Being educated does not necessarily make you wise in other aspects of life. In my community, there is a saying that the level of one's education and a lack in the person's ability is a matter of one's home orientation.

A good example would be the story of Eli and Samuel. When God was calling Samuel, he could not discern who was calling him. Eli's experience made Samuel know who was calling and what to do. There is a need for a relationship between the elders and youth even in our society today. The young have the ability of tech while the older adults have the experience to guide and apply in different aspects of our lives.

❖ The Building Season

The validation of what is learned comes from field experience.

As a youth, you need to be aware that life has seasons. Today, we see the rush in youth to make money without regard to the future implications. Most students would even say education is a fraud because of today's get-rich schemes. I believe this results from the wrong impressions given to individuals about education. How about the self-liberation one gets and the knowledge no one can take from them? If you are well educated, you can start life anywhere in the world and continuously learn to adapt to different systems.

Good things take time, but it is worth every sweat, as the scripture admonishes us not to envy the wicked as their doomsday approaches. Whatever you plant, you will reap, and the same principle applies to life. <u>God builds your character and equips you for the task ahead.</u> It would be best if you were patient and learned to do well all your hands find to do in that season.

6

Education Without Purpose

Chapter 6

Education Without Purpose Is Dangerous

Bishop David Oyedepo said 'Remember, God has defined the purpose of your creation. Until you accept, adapt, and identify with it, you will never be at your best.' Education without purpose stops you from becoming your best. Finding your purpose is the foundation on which you should build your education. Ideally, the pursuit of education should translate into the chase of your objective.

We can look at the purpose of education from two perspectives. One, the purpose driving educational policies and practices influences educational curriculums. This purpose is solely in the power of the government, exercised through the educational ministry. The second perspective on purpose in education is the student's goal for attending school. Every student has two educational purposes to contend with in pursuit of their career.

The problem here is that the government measures education productivity against its purpose. Irrespective of the student's purpose for schooling, the government's purpose is primary and supersedes anything else. Students have to find their purpose within the government purpose. It is a conflicting dilemma that students always face throughout their career years.

If an educational policy is not achieving its purpose, the government changes it without a second thought. Such arbitrary changes often affect students' purpose for schooling, and they have to redefine their goals amidst changes in their educational environment and framework.

Below, I have listed some of the purposes of education proposed by various governments in different countries.

- ✓ **Integration**

The purpose of education has gone through various changes in response to societal needs. From the 1930s to the 1990s, the purpose of education went through a curve of changes. Using the US as a case study of the global pattern, a survey suggested that purpose never remains constant. The suggestion alone presents education as a field of dynamic changes, and students must adapt accordingly to find and fulfill their purpose.

> ***Society has little to benefit from the people's education, except there is room for competition to distinguish intellectual superiority.***

Education in the 1930s focused on developing young people to fit into society. We can refer to this purpose as integration. Different countries and cultures pursued this purpose of education with the singular goal of evolving a harmonious society.

In pursuit of this purpose, some countries have reduced their internal conflicts and cultural barriers. For instance, Canada has pursued this goal to bridge its people's cultural and racial gap. Some aborigines have been able to integrate into a more cohesive and upward moving society of modern Canada. Australia also pursued the same goal, which helped some of her aborigines embrace the larger community's norms and fit better into it.

When a government deems fit to integrate a section, group of people, age bracket, and so on into the mainstream of the society, they evolve educational policies and laws that enforce the purpose. And doing so includes curriculum development and choice of subjects or topics to be taught. You can look at the educational curriculum of a country and understand the purpose the government is trying to achieve with it.

Many governments still style their educational purposes and policies to achieve integration. The present situation in Nigeria's education sector points to integration purposes where the quota system applies to admission requirements. The old belief that some states and people are 'educationally disadvantaged' is why we have unequal, unfair, and unbalanced admission requirements.

In the spirit of integration and nation-building, as the government often argues, some people's career pace and potentials have to slow down or stop for others to catch up. That way, Nigeria can forge ahead as a single society of educational equilibrium. Nothing sets back a country more than an educational purpose with no country's interest as its goal.

✓ Critical Thinking

In the late 1940s, the trend in the purpose of education changed from integration to critical thinking. Countries were dissatisfied with merely integrating members of their societies. After integration and societal cohesion, the question is, what next?

We can see the evolution of education purpose in response to genuine societal needs. Suppose we have a mass of society members with a reasonably good level of education. Society has little to benefit from the people's education, except there is room for competition to distinguish intellectual superiority. This purpose in education does not see education as enough except the educated can prove their worth through critical thinking.

Critical thinking is the process of information analysis, evaluation, interpretation, and application to solve problems. It is a process where these mental activities lead to valuable conclusions. The critical thinking process aims at winning in disputes or conflicts. This purpose of education seeks deeper and richer solutions to societal problems.

You know that a country is yet to achieve this purpose in its education when more certificates are produced than the number of solutions to the nation's problems. Where more legal battles are lost and new legal conflicts emerge, which the array of lawyers in a country cannot handle, it's an indicator that the government is still operating at a level where a certificate is more important than its holder. We can use the exact measurement to judge other professions. The legal profession is not intended to be a scapegoat in my argument.

- ✓ **Morality**

A decade after the introduction of critical thinking, a shift towards morality began to dominate the purpose of education. Developed countries, especially the US, were at the forefront of this move.

Let me point out that as each purpose fulfills its goal, new problems merge, and education must be used as a tool for solving them. Developed countries don't see education as merely going to school to learn how to read and write. They see education as an instrument for national development. Hence, they identify problems they hope education should be able to solve.

For example, do you wonder why Kyoto University, the second-best university in Japan, has Disaster Prevention Research Institute? Japan has seen years of many natural disasters like earthquakes, cyclones, volcanoes, floods, and tsunamis. Each time these disasters hit the country, development, economic and social life is adversely affected. The government education policy and purpose must suit the national interest of disaster prevention and management.

Lack of resourcefulness is why people suffer amid the abundance in their land.

The American educational curriculum has created 'Corrections' as a degree, post-graduate, or Master's programme in many universities. Initially, the course belonged to Psychology, criminology, and criminal justice. America has the highest prison rates and the number of inmates globally. China and Russia follow it.

A country with massive and numerous prison facilities couldn't do any less than formulate education purposes and policies to address the problem. Corrections as programme entails supervision of suspects arrested, convicted, or sentenced for criminal offenses.

In an era where morality was top on the purpose of education, it was believed that critical thinking was not enough without moral uprightness. Before then, society soon discovered that people of high intellect also committed the worst crimes. So they saw the need to combine intelligence with morals for a sane and safe human environment.

- ✓ **Resourcefulness**

Around the mid-1960s, education's purpose tilted towards learning beyond literacy. Literacy is defined as the ability to read and write. Literacy promotes equality across gender, religion, race, and other boundaries of differences that cause discrimination. Learning is different from literacy because it helps one perform a task more efficiently by using available resources.

The purpose education seeks to achieve with this slant is creativity or ingenuity. Anyone who can use available resources to solve a problem is a genius. We can see from this trend that education's purpose was directed towards using available resources in a country to solve the country's problems. That is what proper education does in the life of a nation.

Nigeria is proud to host the second Bitumen deposit in the world after Venezuela, yet it has some of the worst road surfaces and networks globally. Road construction asphalt, roofing materials like the American shingles, waterproofing mechanisms, and others are products derivable from Bitumen. Lack of resourcefulness is why people suffer amid the abundance in their land.

- ✓ **Human Capacity Development**

Experts say the only purpose of education that remains constant over the decades - and which should remain so - is that education should achieve human capacity development. Every educated person must evolve into and stay a complete human being in the real sense of the word.

Any educated person thus behaving less than human is a disappointment to the ultimate purpose of education. Education is worthless if it does not enhance creativity, economic development, social cohesion, religious tolerance, fundamental human rights, and a host of other objectives.

✓ Individual Purpose of Education

Their purpose in education boosts students' high performance. Students with a clear purpose are known to perform better. A purpose-driven education leads to purposeful living.

A reoccurring issue in Nigeria is the choice of education and field of study determined by situations and the environment. The average Nigerian student would settle for a course out of the availability of resources and facilities that a school can provide.

An accurate example of education without purpose is the majority of students who find happiness when there is an opportunity not to attend class.

Although the student in question has a role to play in accepting the given course, most students settle for available programmes due to the high demand for admission. Their decision affects their potential and hinders the more extraordinary minds that would have done great things in the future.

There is a question I might not answer: would it be advisable to turn down this offer if one finds themselves in such a situation. I would say everything is pending on the individuals. In our locality, there is a mindset that studying a financially prospective course is the right thing to do, which most parents and students believe. Individuals differ, and while this might work for some, it may not work for others. Again, we are different, and so are our purpose and assignment here on earth.

In most of his books, Myles Monroe mentioned, "When a purpose for a thing is not known, abuse is inevitable." This fact tells us that everything is created for a purpose, and finding purpose in education is no different if we want to live a fulfilled life.

An accurate example of education without purpose is the majority of students who find happiness when there is an opportunity not to attend class. Education has a stipulated time assigned to it. Those enthusiastic about their course portray different attitudes to school activities compared to those whiling away time with school. The training in schools of education would not be maximized when the candidate does not know the purpose of the education. This experience is predominant in most institutions today.

> **Ecclesiastes 9:10:**
> *Whatever you do, do it well. For when you go to the grave, there will be no work, planning, knowledge, or wisdom.*

The principle of seed and harvest will not favour you when you study without purpose. Not knowing the reason for your education will always put you at a disadvantage. Your determination and perseverance to always become better will enhance your ability to excel.

The quality of the seed will determine the outcome of the product. When you study to pass an examination, you will leave with just a certificate. But when you learn to make something out of education, you will go with a certificate and extra skills that others lack. What distinguishes and sets you apart is the extra quality you possess besides your certificate. No certificate is enough on its own.

An illustration of the 'not enough' certificate theory is a trip I made with my best friend. We made a sightseeing trip. It was spectacular but with lots of confusion. I had never been that confused in my life. I could not think or even sort out a single problem in my head. Everything seemed so blurry that I decided to tell my friend, Cremelda, to help with most thinking.

We traveled without sorting essential things like our interlinking destinations, flights, and accommodation. We knew that we were travelling from Copenhagen, Denmark, to the United Kingdom, Switzerland, Geneva, Barcelona, Madrid, Spain, and back to London. And from London, we were to continue the trip to Liverpool, Manchester, and back to Malmö, Sweden, for graduation.

Our trip was filled with adventures and fear of the unknown. Most of the places were unfamiliar, and most people we met could not speak English because our destinations were French and Spanish-speaking nations. But as the way God would do His stuff (that's an optimist Nigerian language), we met friendly people.

We met people with kids that would go any length to put us on the right routes. We also met people coming back from work tired. Despite being unlikely to help, they gave us attention and provided us with direction and descriptions.

Before I forget, our first destination was in the UK to drop off some luggage for shipping back to Sierra Leone, my friend's home country. The last shipment for the year to Sierra Leone was due on the 26th of October 2017.

I had booked our trip from Copenhagen to Manchester instead of London. When I got the news, we decided to get the train from Manchester to London after our arrival, but a single ticket was worth one hundred and sixty-five (£165) pounds to our surprise. We were not pleased, but we both kept mute.

My friend said she would not have traveled with her luggage to get to the platform because it was not worth the cost. I then proceeded to see if it could change the ticket from London to Liverpool. I met the ticketer, and she changed it for us and gave us the refunds of the extra cash.

You needed to see the deep breath I took and the warm smile on my face at that point. My friend and I acknowledged that the price was excessively high, and if we had gone on the trip, we would not have been happy with ourselves. We finally sent the box parcel for thirteen pounds through UPS to London from Liverpool.

We stayed with my friend in Liverpool, who turned out to be as welcoming as a sister but left the next day. Another incident worth mentioning happened on the day we left Liverpool. Before the trip, I made some orders of books I was planning to take back home to Nigeria to keep myself busy for the National Youth service year ahead.

The books were to be delivered to my friend, Comfort but were brought when she wasn't around. I had to pick them up because my name was on the orders, but I needed to show proof of identification with my name and photograph on it.

After going through the process, we sent the luggage the same day and picked up my orders. We had to make our way to Manchester from Liverpool. My friend, Comfort, decided to help take us to Manchester in her car. Her decision was quite touching because she had two children to take care of.

The last baby was just seven months then, but regardless, she took us on this journey. The weather was awful, and it was the peak hour when the highway was busy as people were going back home from their various destinations.

∞

There is power in education pursued with purpose.

We finally arrived at the airport and successfully boarded the plane. We thought we would miss it at some point, but we made it. We had already booked accommodation from Manchester airport to Geneva, Switzerland, while in Liverpool that night. Hotels were too expensive; we then used Airbnb and got one within our budget.

When we got to Geneva, we discovered our accommodation was in France. Unknown to us, France and Switzerland share a border. We arrived at night and had to ask people around for directions. The bus that would have taken us to France had closed for the day.

The tram became the only option left. Someone from there decided we should follow him. We took a bus from the central station in Geneva after getting the ticket, stopped at some point, and changed to tram service.

The above story, to me, shows what the journey of education could be. It could be rough and laborious, and it could be a long, winding journey to the final destination. You will get to your career destination if you don't give up. On the trip, separate events occurred on the way. Some threatened the result we hoped to get, but along the way, solutions were found through the help of Good Samaritans.

You need all these experiences for the journey ahead. Some will give up on the trip. Those with purpose will keep moving while others engage with distractions and fail to make it through to their goals. <u>There is power in education pursued with purpose.</u>

7

The Importance Of career Guide

Chapter 7

The Importance of Career Guide

Career guide or counseling has lost its place in Nigeria's educational system. In many public and private schools, a career counselor's office is non-existent. Those still practicing the noble profession have offices, outlets, or platforms outside the school system.

A career guide or counseling can be defined as a profession that helps students with guidelines on choosing appropriate programs of study. But career counseling does more than that. It also allows students to change or leave one program for another after an objective evaluation of their potential, weaknesses, strengths, and passions.

Career counseling is a process that leads students to self-discovery. The profession recognizes students' ability variations and performance tendencies in specific areas of students. It advises them accordingly and encourages them to make decisions that best suit their personalities and potential. The death of professional career guidance and counseling in elementary and secondary schools creates a vacuum of vagueness in students' career paths.

> *Career guide or counseling has lost its place in Nigeria's educational system.*

Students' career misadventure begins with wrong career choices. These students pursue academic programmes they are not passionate about all their lives. They stand no chance of benefitting their lives or the society with their careers. The absence of a career guide or counsel makes a country produce graduates who become misfits in whatever field they are found.

Lack of career guidance and counseling is a source of mental, emotional, and health hazards in the students' life. Students in the wrong careers go through so much stress. Stress is a gateway to anxiety, and anxiety is the last door to depression. Education's purpose is not only defeated by a lack of career guidance; the student's life on a wrong career path is in danger.

Choosing a career is not as easy as it sounds. Students have to be sincere when answering questions during their career guide. Self-delusion is to say 'yes' when the answer is 'no.' A career counselor can help draw essential questions to help the student's choice. Left alone, the students may not know all the questions they should ask and answer. Many students are on career paths for the pride belonging there.

Common questions to answer in deciding a career choice include the following:

- ✓ What do I find easy to do?
- ✓ What do I like to do?
- ✓ What gives me fulfillment?
- ✓ What skills stand me out?
- ✓ What does my attention span look like?
- ✓ Am I better with figures than words?
- ✓ Am I better with words than figures?
- ✓ Am I an introvert?
- ✓ Am I an extrovert?
- ✓ Do I like adventures?
- ✓ Do I hate taking risks?
- ✓ Do I tend to act before thinking?
- ✓ Do I tend to think before acting?

- ✓ Do I enjoy difficult tasks?
- ✓ Do I hate and avoid difficult tasks?

Education involves critical decision-making. Unfortunately, in this part of the world, career guide is non-functional. I remember the dilemma of choosing which university to fill in my jamb form. Funny enough, I knew how ignorant I was in that phase.

I did ask questions, but nobody gave me a satiable answer; instead, I was made to believe it was a choice I had to make. However, it is worth noting that I have never had the opportunity to be introduced to career paths or universities that offer such courses.

❖ I Wanted To Be A Doctor

Choosing a career is not as easy as it sounds.

As a child, I only wanted medicine because doctors are perceived to be very smart and intelligent, and for the fact that I love solving problems. I spent most of my primary holidays helping the elderly around me, encouraging and assisting where their strength failed them.

Nevertheless, it only became so glaring that I empathized with whoever had challenges as I grew. When a friend of mine became pregnant, I could not help but join in planning how to put things in place for the baby's arrival. A much older person advised me to wait for the baby's arrival before buying the clothing, but I could not just wait for them. Who knows what would have been the result of that journey.

The scholarship I have to study nautical science opened another path for me. The struggle was real because I could not help but question how ignorant the student in my area was during my first days in school. I never thought about ships or was curious about what happens there.

During my higher diploma, bachelor and Master's degree, the exposure I got remains the best thing that changed my life. What I ended up studying is something I never thought of or imagined.

After the two phases of nautical science scholarship, the next phase was the sea training, which I opted out of the programme not because I could not, but because when I thought about my long-term plans, I did not see myself sailing for life. I had come far, and it would only be wise, so I thought then to study something in the same field that would enable me to work in an office.

This decision was hard, joining the crowd to prove a point or urge something else. At the time, I felt the consequences of both decisions even though it was not easy. I did further for a bachelor's degree at Liverpool John Moores University, where I did Maritime Business and Management, but at the end of the degree, I felt the same void, more like it was nothing. I travelled back home and discussed the option of furthering my Master's.

After deciding to further my Master's, I wondered if I had made the right decision. The more doubt set into my heart, the more the fear of the unknown I had to face. I decided to risk vulnerability for God to take His place. Due to the kind of family I hail from, I could not voice it to anyone but myself. I finally embarked on the Master's degree in Malmö, Sweden.

I thanked God and my family for allowing me to see all that I set my eyes on and have the chance to meet people from several nations, cultures, backgrounds, and beliefs all over the world, plus the several field study trips awaiting us. This phase was and still is the best time of my life.

Education involves critical decision-making.

With the entire certificate, I knew my education was only making it possible for me to excel in a particular field but not in life at large. What it takes to be successful, why some people are rich, and others are not, could not stop ringing in my mind. However, I understood that success is relative.

For some, certificates would be a dream-come-true, but they are essential only for job search. I believe there is more to my life than just my education.

Education is a means of acquiring knowledge, skills, and experience to solve life problems. It is essential to know that not every problem is a general problem for everyone. The same thing is with the individual flare to solve particular problems.

A post on Instagram by @Ibukunawosika on the 12th of May 2021 better explains the point, saying, 'according to a book written by Marcus Buckingham and Donald O. Clifton states, "every person is capable of doing something better than the following 10,000 people."' Their book titled 'Now, Discover Your Strength' encourages everyone to find their strength and make the most of it.

Imagine competing with someone already in a field of strength combined with hard work; the sky would indeed be the starting point. You have no chance in such a race. Education has its place, and finding your strength has its place as well. It is not supposed to be a stroll to attain just a certificate. It is a place where new births occur when combined with the right ingredients.

Education is a means of acquiring knowledge, skills, and experience to solve life problems.

According to Myles Munroe, every individual born on earth has an inherent gift that enables them to carry out their assignment. Your distinction comes when you discover your strength and talent and acquire the knowledge that better equips you to carry out your tasks effectively.

About The Author

Imorataria Dogood Akpufu is a Lecturer at the department of Port Management, Nigeria Maritime University (NMU), Okerenkoko, Delta State, Nigeria. She holds two HNCs in Natural Sciences from UK & India; a BSc in Maritime Business & Management (UK). She also holds a Master's degree in Port Management (Sweden) with a PhD in view along with at least eight training and professional certificates from India and Singapore coupled with many awards and memberships. She firmly believes in originality and purpose.

Taria, as the author is fondly called, is a service and solution-driven individual with her fair share of burnout from trying to fit into a box. She is on a mission to eradicate unproductive education; with a vision to training productive youth through mind-set alteration.

The expectations of people basically are the standard she would live to. Just like plant do not want soil but needs it, the same became her frustration and the only way out of these situations knowing how insatiable human beings can be, she needed something far bigger than what she has experienced so far.

On this journey of self-realisation are lessons learnt along the way, that shows More light, the consequences and the necessity of making this journey far better and interesting for other upcoming individuals that will yield greater results both in the academics and in their personal life spaces.

www.ingramcontent.com/pod-product-compliance
Lightning Source LLC
LaVergne TN
LVHW012116170826
845678LV00014BA/2967